D0627329

The cats that love to snap (and chat)

ROSIE RYDER

SNAPCAT

Copyright © Summersdale Publishers Ltd, 2017

All rights reserved.

No part of this book may be reproduced by any means, nor transmitted, nor translated into a machine language, without the written permission of the publishers.

Condition of Sale
This book is sold subject to the condition that it shall not, by way of trade or otherwise, be lent, resold, hired out or otherwise circulated in any form of binding or cover other than that in which it is published and without a similar condition including this condition being imposed on the subsequent purchaser.

Summersdale Publishers Ltd
46 West Street
Chichester
West Sussex
PO19 1RP
UK

www.summersdale.com

Printed and bound in China

ISBN: 978-1-78685-343-1

Substantial discounts on bulk quantities of Summersdale books are available to corporations, professional associations and other organisations. For details contact general enquiries: telephone: +44 (0) 1243 771107, fax: +44 (0) 1243 786300 or email: enquiries@summersdale.com.

10 9 8 7 6 5 4 3 2 1

Disclaimer
This book is not endorsed by, promoted by or associated with Snapchat ™.

Meet the snapcats

So, you thought it was only humans who were hooked on Snapchat? Well, think again – we have evidence to the contrary. These are the cats who live in the moment, snapping the world around them and sharing their stories with their feline friends.

These cool kitties have a lot to say, and whether it's with a cheeky sticker or a sassy caption, they say it with style. Find out what they get up to when we're not looking, discover what they're really thinking and prepare to see your fur-miliar friends through a whole new lens…

Looks like someone's had a rough day

Float
like a 🦋,
sting like a
🐝

dat ass tho

heck

Selfie Queen #nofilter

#proteingoals

So busted 😂

It's bathtime

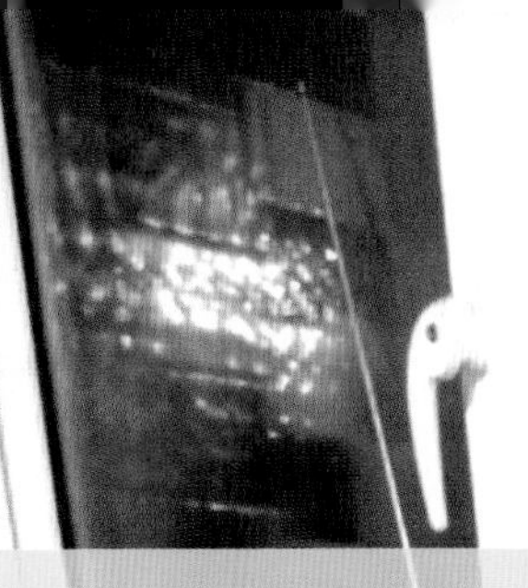

Heard u were talkin trash

Shame on you,
Mittens

Help i have fallen

How you doin'?

#tantrums

He's just planning my assassination NBD

Whatever floats ur boat I guess...

We accept the presents
we think we deserve

When u know u should do something useful but u could also sit and do nothing

That's one
Jason Bourne
MF

When ur done adulting for the day

When he tells u to smile

Someone ate his snacks again

The truth is out there

She thinks she’s people

Sweet air guitar solo

When u accidentally open the front facing camera

i do what i want susan

CAN U NOT

When the alarm clock says morning
but u still feel like last night

I sense a disturbance in the force

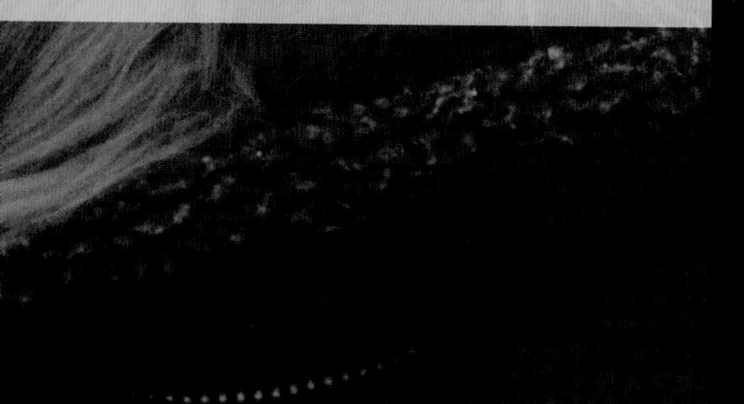

Nora, cancel my
2 o'clock

TFW ur 500% done with clean eating

chillaxing

#slay

Someone just offered him a chicken nugget 🍗

They're ironic

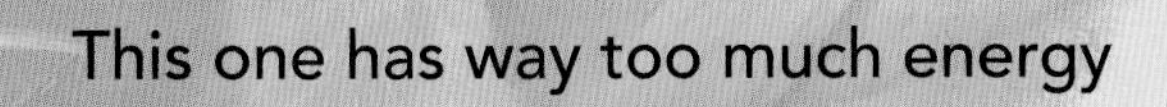
This one has way too much energy

Aw yiss

BFFs 4eva

Bae caught me slippin

She's sexy an she know it

UGH
Monday...

Wen u try ur best but u dont succeed

This could be us
but u playin

She knows it’s the vet

One day he's gonna turn on us all.

1st January

The risk I took was calculated
but man am I bad at math

Spidey sense is tingling

ladies

Bueno

Snap me like one of ur French girls

o shoot

Twerking...

MEOW

Just look at this creeper

If I fits,
I sits

Hi this is tom I stole meg's phone lol

When u know he's seen ur message but hasn't replied

Chins 4 dayz

u ok hun?

Wouldn’t mess with this one if I were you

#foodbaby

Dayum girl
werk

He's plotting something shady I know it.

Problems = 99

Majestic AF.

Hello, this is cat

Soon...

Looks like Marvin's gonna need fixing again

Life is hard.

javaaa

The Creation of Cat

u came 2
da wrong
neighborhood

BYE
When u hear the bath water runnin

H8rs gonna h8

#floof

Barbara do u mind?

Waddup

Suck it,
Schrödinger.

Party don’t start till I walk in

Pretty sure someone’s plotting my death

She loved
me once...

i woke up
like dis

Get in loser we’re going shopping

my precious

#relationshipgoals

Waiting for tinderella

#hygge

When ur parents have guests round and u just want something from the kitchen.

I have the best hair. It's terrific.
Everyone agrees.

me gusta

Netflix n chill turned into netflix n snooze

This seat is taken 🚫

What a poser

Trying to get through the week like...

NOPE

zzz

I read *The Girl on the Train*
before it was cool

Carbs is love

Slidin into ur snaps like

All around me are familiar faces...

Houston she has seen the treats

u kids keep it down ok

Boop

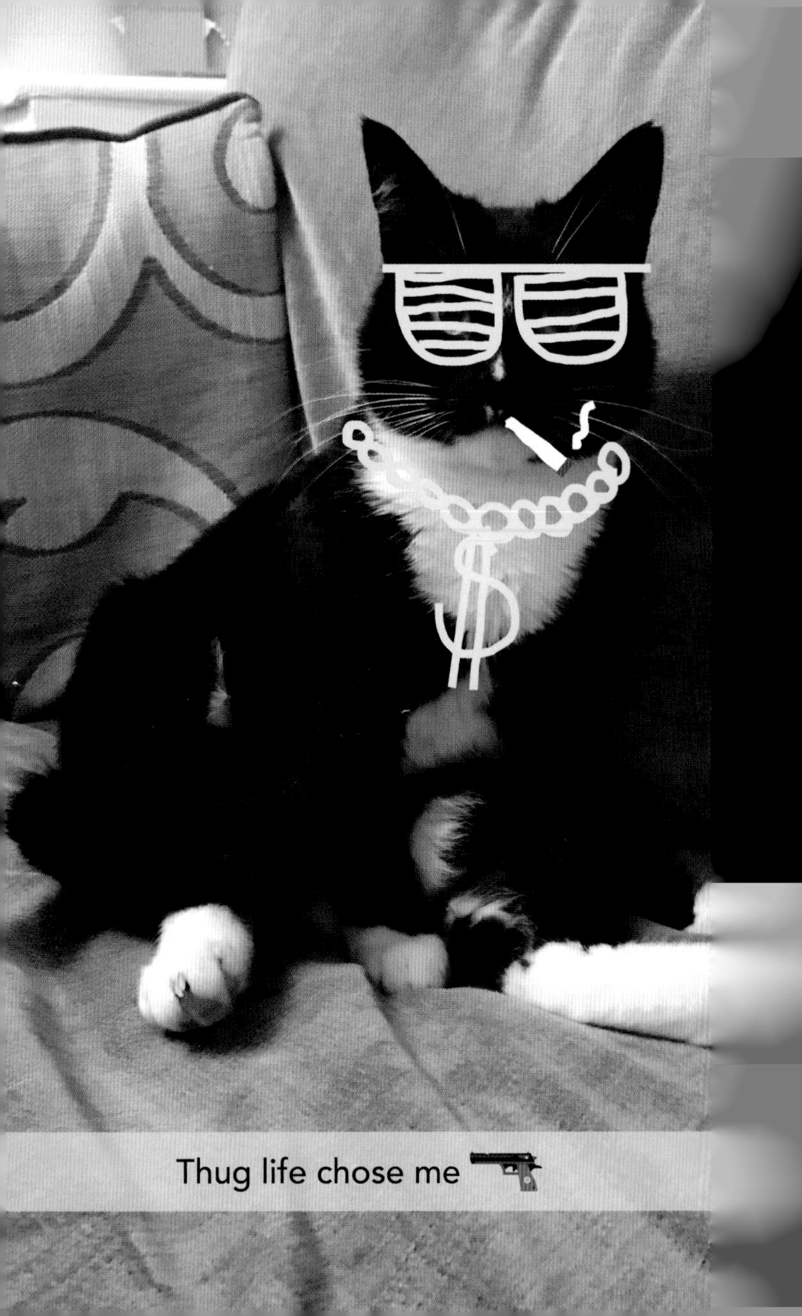
Thug life chose me

When ur mom gets u ready
for the first day of school

Tell me about ur childhood

So close yet so far

Okay get a room guys

Fierce but cute

Bestie

Send help

Bae 1,
personal space 0

Yaaaaaaassss!

Who run da worl

Photo Credits

p.4 Betty © Belle Clarke
p.5 © Marie Charouzova
p.6 © DavidTB
p.7 © Dennis van de Water
p.8 Tango © Keira Manley
p.9 Lillie © Sarah & Jonny Ball
p.10 © DarkBird
p.11 Indy © Tom & Amy Wilkins
p.12 Tilly © Ellie Young
p.13 Luna © Chris Turton & Amanda Carter
p.14 © kuban_girl
p.15 © vvvita
p.16 Freddie © David Eccles
p.17 © Anna Hoychuk
p.18 Kaymak © Nazli Gurkas
p.19 Larry © Hannah May
p.20 Wizard © Helen Frost
p.21 Lillie © Sarah & Jonny Ball
p.22 © mishanik_210
p.23 Tango © Keira Manley
p.24 Mookie © Mark Bolt
p.25 Lewis © Anita Zih
p.26 © Anya Sam
p.27 © GooDween123
p.28 Poppy © Ellie Young
p.29 Kaymak © Nazli Gurkas
p.30 Tilly © Ellie Young
p.31 © staoist520
p.32 Tigger © Liz Rich
p.33 © DavidTB
p.34 Luna © Chris Turton & Amanda Carter
p.35 Biber © Nazli Gurkas
p.36 © Astrid Gast
p.37 © Zanna Holstova
p.38 Tilly © Ellie Young
p.39 © Pap Kutasi Szilvia
p.40 © SVPhilon
p.41 © Zanna Holstova
p.42 © kaminov74
p.43 Ginger © Nova Black-stock
p.44 © TungCheung
p.45 Indiana & Miel © Lara & Terry Hancock
p.46 Tango © Keira Manley
p.47 © Lapina
p.48 Walter © Claire Plimmer
p.49 © BrAt82
p.50 © Steve Collender
p.51 © Julie A Lynch
p.52 © Silver30
p.53 © foaloce
p.54 ©JASPERIMAGE
p.55 Sooty © Steve & Gemma Brownlee
p.56 © Andrzej Tarnawczyk
p.57 © Popel Arseniy
p.58 Rosie © Sarah Ball
p.59 © Sergey Smolentsev
p.60 © BlackRabbit3
p.61 © Renata Apanaviciene
p.62 © Chendongshan
p.63 © Art_man
p.64 © Renata Apanaviciene
p.65 © Courtney A Denning
p.66 © karamysh
p.67 Lillie © Sarah & Jonny Ball
p.68 Mookie & Luna © Mark Bolt
p.69 Lillie © Sarah & Jonny Ball

p.70 Wizard © Helen Frost
p.71 © Tony Campbell
p.72 © Joanna22
p.73 © NicO_l
p.74 © Svetlana Batalina
p.75 © Zanna Holstova
p.76 Rosie © Sarah Ball
p.77 © WindNight
p.78 Missy & Archie © Lauren Nickless & Dan Morgans
p.79 Lillie © Sarah & Jonny Ball
p.80 © Kike Fernandez
p.81 © Sari ONeal
p.82 Sooty © Steve & Gemma Brownlee
p.83 © createthis
p.84 © Nailia Schwarz
p.85 © Petrenko Andriy
p.86 © C Salisbury
p.87 © Tan Chuan-Yean
p.88 © amenic181
p.89 Mickey © Kerry & Andy Williams
p.90 Indiana © Lara & Terry Hancock
p.91 Missy © Lauren Nickless & Dan Morgans
p.92 © alexytrener
p.93 Lillie © Sarah & Jonny Ball
p.94 © Tonhom1009
p.95 © DreamBig
p.96 Indiana & Miel © Lara & Terry Hancock
p.97 © Suzanne Tucker
p.98 © Tatyana Domnicheva
p.99 © BrAt82
p.100 © JeepFoto
p.101 © Ewais
p.102 © Ivan Tsvetkov
p.103 © Muhammad Ahsan Iqbal
p.104 Indy © Tom & Amy Wilkins
p.105 Indiana & Miel © Lara & Terry Hancock
p.106 © kuban_girl
p.107 © moonraiter82
p.108 © SUSAN LEGGETT
p.109 © Dmitrij Skorobogatov
p.110 © Stephen Jingel
p.111 © Dmitrijs Kaminskis
p.112 © Sharnikau Uladzimir
p.113 © DavidTB
p.114 Mickey © Kerry & Andy Williams
p.115 © TalyaPhoto
p.116 © vvvita
p.117 Rosie © Sarah Ball
p.118 Ginger © Nova Black-stock
p.119 © NorthernLand
p.120 © Suzanne Tucker
p.121 © Patrick Lienin
p.122 Dusty & Angus © Jill Farlow
p.123 Lillie © Sarah & Jonny Ball
p.124 © Borkin Vadim
p.125 Larry © Hannah May

All credits in which the cat is not referred to by its name are the joint copyright of the image holder and Shutterstock.

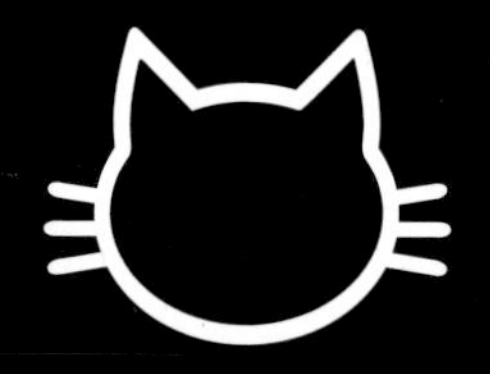

If you're interested in finding out
more about our books, find us on Facebook
at **Summersdale Publishers** and follow
us on Twitter at **@Summersdale**.

www.summersdale.com